A Salute to Historic Blacks in Government

Copyright © 1990, 1996 by Empak Publishing Company

ISBN 0-922162-9-3 (Volume IX)
ISBN 0-922162-15-8 (Volume Set)

A Salute to Historic Blacks in Government

EMPAK PUBLISHING COMPANY

Publisher & Editor: Richard L. Green
Senior Editor: Sylvia Shepherd
Researcher: Sylvia Shepherd
Production: Dickinson & Associates, Inc.
Illustration: S. Gaston Dobson
Preface: Empak Publishing Co.

PREFACE

Each of the distinguished men and women in this booklet, *A Salute to Blacks in the Federal Government,* represent political power at the national level. They held high positions, both elective and appointive. Some served in Congress, and others responded to Presidential summons. They excelled in positions that symbolized the power that America highly regards, political power. And, each of the notable individuals reported upon understood the significance of this power as a catalyst for progressive change.

Many of the people presented in this booklet were prominent in other fields, such as Richard Cain, who was an African Methodist Episcopal Church bishop, and James Milton Turner, who was an educator. Most were prominent in state legislatures before moving up to the national scene. The Blacks included in this booklet represent only a small portion of those who chose politics as a path of endeavor. The exception to the abundance of early Black achievers is the relatively small group of women represented. This attests to the fact that Black women were denied even longer the opportunity to participate in the political process.

Well represented are Blacks of the Reconstruction era, that period after the Civil War when, for a brief and remarkable time, Blacks Republicans were granted political power. During this period, more than 20 Blacks were elected to Congress from the South. This era was deplorably short-lived as southern White Democrats found ways to disenfranchise Blacks once again.

In recent decades, though, Blacks have impressively returned to the local, state and national political scene. They are working within the Democratic and Republican parties once again and are writing new chapters in Black History. As in every political post, both past and present—Black politicians have had to struggle on two fronts—for their own self-survival and for the advancement of their race. The biographies in this booklet convey that Black politicians have been optimistic even in the face of extreme difficulties and obstructions. Their stories demonstrate how hard work and vision lifted them above the masses and molded them into persons ready for new and broad responsibility.

Few Americans are fully aware of the long history of Black political participation which has transpired within the political arena of the United States. *A Salute to Blacks in Federal Government*, like the others in the EMPAK series, is dedicated to underscore, highlight, and circumvent what one writer called "the three D's": distortion, deletion and denial of Black accomplishments in U.S. history. For all these reasons, EMPAK is proud to add this title to its growing list of Black History volumes.

Empak Publishing Company

CONTENTS

*Editor's Note: Due to this booklet's space limitations, some facts on the lives
of the above noted Blacks in the Federal Government have
been omitted.*

EBENEZER D. BASSETT
(1833 - 1908)

Our country's first Black diplomat, Ebenezer D. Bassett, performed his duties so well in an internationally sensitive assignment that he became dean of the American diplomatic corps. His success led the way to appointments of other Blacks to ministerial posts in the Caribbean and Africa.

Bassett was born in Litchfield, Connecticut, in 1833, to a mulatto, Tobias Bassett, and a Pequot tribe Indian, Susan. He studied at Wesley Academy in Massachusetts and was graduated with honors from Connecticut State Normal School. While working as a high school principal in New Haven, Connecticut, Bassett continued his studies at Yale College.

In 1855, Bassett married Eliza Park, and they had two daughters and three sons. Two years after his marriage, Bassett became principal of the Institute for Colored Youth in Philadelphia, a Quaker school to train Blacks to be teachers. He proved himself a multi-talented instructor, teaching natural sciences, mathematics, and classics, while serving as school librarian.

Bassett was equally successful as a school administrator, with the mayor of Philadelphia referring to the school as "widely known and unquestionably the foremost institution of its kind in the country." Bassett held this post until 1869, when President Ulysses S. Grant appointed him minister to Haiti and the Dominican Republic, two countries which share an island south of Florida. Bassett's selection was based on letters of recommendation from prominent Americans, including his Yale professors, who wrote of their high regard for him. His study of French, at Yale, was an important help in his ministerial duties in the Caribbean.

When Bassett arrived in Port-au-Prince, Haiti, the situation was tense. The United States was considering the annexation of the Dominican Republic to protect American shipping in the Caribbean. Haitians opposed the annexation, fearing that Haiti also would be annexed. Meanwhile, Haiti had serious internal problems. During Bassett's service on the island, one Haitian president was shot, another was forced to flee the country, and another sought political refuge in the minister's residence. Through it all, Bassett served the United States "with honor to himself and satisfaction to his country." Before his resignation in 1877, he had also been elected to the presidency of the exclusive "Cercle de Port-au-Prince."

Bassett's involvement with Haiti continued. Beginning in 1879, he served for 10 years as Haiti's Consul General in New York City. After that, he moved to Haiti and lived there for four years. During this time, Frederick Douglass took over as United States minister to Haiti and the Dominican Republic and Bassett worked for Douglass as an interpreter and secretary. According to Douglass, Hamilton Fish, the United States Secretary of State, "wished one-half of his ministers abroad performed their duties as well as Mr. Bassett."

In 1892, Bassett and his family returned to the United States, where he wrote the *Handbook of Haiti*, which was printed in English, French, and Spanish. For this achievement, he was named a member of the American Geographical Society and the Connecticut Historical Society.

Bassett spent his last years in Philadelphia with his family. During his stay in Haiti, he had contracted a tropical disease, malaria, dengue, or both. His last letter to Douglass, dated back to January 1894, while Bassett was still working, complained of "an annoying affection of my eyes which are never in good trim." In 1908, he died in Philadelphia. But his well-regarded works survive in his written *Handbook*, in the papers of Frederick Douglass, and in the diplomatic correspondence in our National Archives.

EDWARD W. BROOKE
(1919 -   )

When Massachusetts voters elected Edward W. Brooke to the U.S. Senate in 1966, they voted on his record, not his race. If race had been a determining factor, Brooke would never have become the first elected Black U.S. senator in our history. In Massachusetts, Blacks accounted for less than five percent of the voters.

Born in 1919, in Washington, D.C., Edward Brooke was named after his father, a Veterans Administration lawyer for 50 years, and his grandfather. His mother, Helen Seldon Brooke, influenced her son with her religious faith and spirited determination. Planning on a career in medicine, Brooke entered Howard University in Washington, where both his father and older sister attended. Graduating in 1941, his undergraduate pursuit, however, had made him uncertain about a medical career.

Brooke was immediately called to World War II duty as a Second Lieutenant. As a member of the all-Black 366th Combat Infantry Regiment, his duties included legally defending enlisted men in court. Brooke soon found himself drawn to his father's profession, law. But, his regiment was shipped overseas and into combat duty. Brooke's regiment invaded Italy, and he won a Bronze Star for heroism. Because of his light skin, curly hair, and knowledge of the Italian language, he masqueraded as an Italian and infiltrated enemy lines.

After the victory in Europe and before Brooke was sent back home, he took a seaside vacation on a beach near Naples, Italy. There, he met Remigia Ferrari Scacco, daughter of an Italian paper merchant. Their two-year correspondence later led to marriage and two daughters.

Brooke graduated from Boston University Law School in 1948. No sooner had he earned a master of laws degree, two of his wartime friends convinced Brooke to run for the Massachusetts state legislature. This was the beginning of a decade of political disappointment, personal and professional growth for Brooke. In 1950, he was defeated in his try for the state legislature. In 1952, he lost his bid to be a general court judge. For eight years, he put politics on a shelf and became engrossed in civic organizations and his law practice.

In 1960, Brooke ran for Massachusetts Secretary of State. Once again, he lost. But he became chairman of the Boston Finance Commission and made a name for himself as a crusader against corruption. Finally, in 1962, he won an election by a margin of 260,000 votes, and became State Attorney General. His work as a effective crime-buster continued and he was re-elected. In 1966, by this time a statewide symbol of honesty, Brooke became the first Black to sit in the U.S. Senate in this century. He won his seat by a margin of over 400,000 votes.

From his Senate seat, Brooke fought for an end to housing bias and for the passage of the 1968 *Civil Rights Act*. He served on President Johnson's Commission on Civil Disorders, as a result of the 1967 ghetto riots. He was part of the successful fight against two U.S. Supreme Court nominees by President Richard Nixon. He was also the first Republican senator to call for Nixon's resignation.

Since leaving the Senate in 1979, Brooke has practiced law and received over 30 honorary degrees. When he accepted the NAACP's Spingarn Medal in 1967, Brooke said, "Those of us who serve in the Congress have a duty to lead, not simply to follow public reaction. We must do more than mirror the present fears and antagonisms of the electorate. We must do what we believe to be legally and morally right."

BLANCHE KELSO BRUCE
(1841 - 1898)

No Black lived a more diverse life than Blanche Kelso Bruce, who started as a field slave and became a United States Senator. This man, who once hid from authorities as a runaway, later mixed with Washington's elite. Though the Reconstruction era improved opportunities for Blacks, Bruce's actual climb to prominence was fueled by his intelligence and ambition.

Bruce was born a slave on a Farmville, Virginia, plantation in 1841. He was the youngest of 11 children to Polly, a slave owned by Pettus Perkinson. Bruce received his early education from the tutor of his master's son. He also worked in a tobacco field and factory. In 1861, Bruce escaped to the free state of Kansas. While there, he started an elementary school for Blacks in the state. After the Civil War, he studied at Oberlin (Ohio) College until lack of money forced him to take a job as a porter on a Mississippi river boat.

In 1869, Bruce heard that Mississippi was a good state for Blacks; so he went there with only 75 cents in his pocket. His energy and attractive personality enabled him climb the ladder of public service. He worked as tax assessor, sheriff, school superintendent and alderman. He also bought a plantation, and rose to importance in the state's Republican Party.

The Mississippi State legislature elected Bruce to the U.S. Senate in 1874, and he took his seat in the nation's highest legislative body when barely 34 years old. Bruce campaigned hard for his Senate seat. Once in Washington, he considered himself a spokesman for his race. Bruce, as head of a Senate Investigation Committee, was responsible for the return of millions of dollars to Black depositors in the bankrupt Freedman's Savings and Trust Company. He constantly introduced bills that would aid Blacks. Each time, he saw White majorities deny his proposals. A bill to desegregate the army was defeated, as were bills to support Black industrial education, and payments to Black soldiers and sailors.

In a Senate executive session, Bruce denounced President Ulysses S. Grant for not caring about Southern Blacks. When Grant summoned him to the White House, he refused to go. Because of his empathy for the treatment of minorities, Bruce also fought for the causes of both Orientals and Indians. In 1878, Bruce married Josephine B. Wilson, a schoolteacher and daughter of a Cleveland dentist. Their son, Roscoe Conkling Bruce, would later be graduated Phi Beta Kappa from Harvard University.

At the Republican National Convention of 1880, Bruce reversed his opinion of Grant and supported him for President. He was temporarily chairing the convention when he recognized the Ohio delegate, James A. Garfield. Garfield's popularity and persuasiveness impressed the other delegates and led to his nomination for the Presidency. Bruce received eight votes for Vice President.

After his Senate term ended in 1881, Bruce received a number of political appointments, becoming Registrar of the Treasury, Recorder of Deeds, and Treasury Registrar once again. He refused appointment as minister to Brazil because that country still had slavery. The Bruce family lived well on his lecture fees, government salary, investments, and a real estate agency.

In 1898, Bruce died of diabetes. At the time of his death, he was hailed for his "tireless zeal" and "unconquerable ambition." He rose from slavery, struggled for an education, spent years in public service, and succeeded as a plantation owner. He sat in the nation's highest legislative body, where he earned the respect of his peers.

YVONNE BRATHWAITE BURKE
(1932 -)

She was attractive, intelligent and aspiring. Only two factors were against young Yvonne Watson. She was Black, and she was a woman. Her goals were ambitious, but prevailing prejudice kept them at bay.

Yvonne was born in 1932, in Los Angeles, to James Watson, an MGM movie studio janitor and union official, and Lola Moore Watson, a real estate agent. She grew up in what she later called "an integrated slum with lots of yards and trees." It was not an easy time to be young. First, there was the greatest economic depression ever suffered by Americans. Then there were the years of World War II.

The Watsons, however, had dreams for their daughter. Willing to sacrifice for their only child, they gave her lessons in music, dancing and speech. Her exceptional brightness gained her entrance into a school operated by the University of Southern California, where she was the only Black.

While still quite young, Yvonne decided to become a lawyer. A scholarship from her father's union enabled her to attend the University of California. The scholarship did not cover all expenses, so she worked in a college library and a garment factory. After earning a bachelor's degree in political science, she enrolled in the University of Southern California School of Law. Her money problems eased somewhat when she got a job as a model. Because the campus women's law society was closed to Blacks and Jews, Yvonne joined two Jewish students to organize a new legal sorority open to all.

In 1956, Burke earned her law degree and passed the California state bar. In the 1950s, racial and sex discrimination was prevalent. Occupations dominated by men would often allow only a token number of women into their ranks. Opportunities were even more limited for Black women. So, she went into private practice, specializing in civil law cases.

In 1957, she married Louis Brathwaite, a mathematician, and continued to practice law and work in various local government jobs. When her seven-year marriage ended, she took her first step into politics as a volunteer with the 1964 Presidential campaign of Lyndon Johnson and Hubert Humphrey.

Two years later, Yvonne defeated six White men in the Democratic primary race for the State's General Assembly. Although called a Communist and a Black militant, she won the election, beating an ultra-conservative Republican. During her three terms in the California State Legislature, she introduced many social welfare bills. She supported prison reform, federal aid to education, equal rights for women, and child care for the disadvantaged.

In 1972, Brathwaite ran for Congress, beating five people in the Democratic primary, and a conservative Republican in the November election. That same year, she became the first Black woman elected to Congress from California, and she married William A. Burke, a Los Angeles businessman. She also gained national attention by serving as Vice-Chairman of the Democratic National Convention in July 1972. While presiding over a portion of the unruly convention, she remained outwardly calm and in control.

During her first term in Washington, Burke gave birth to a daughter, Autumn. She kept up her busy congressional service, consistently working for laws that would help disadvantaged Americans. Burke voted for minimum wage and social security increases, job training for divorced or separated young mothers, a rape crisis center, extended unemployment compensation, and a wide variety of other social programs.

Retired from Congress in 1979, Yvonne Brathwaite Burke could look back at the success achieved against the incredible odds of mid-century America.

RICHARD H. CAIN
(1825 - 1887)

Although the ministry was Richard H. Cain's chief calling in life, his abilities were mainly employed in assisting Blacks in the political arena. Serving in the South as a missionary to his people, he would eventually fight their battles in the U.S. House of Representatives.

Cain was born in 1825, in Greenbrier County, Virginia, to a Black father and an Indian mother. When he was 6 years old, his father took him to Ohio, where they lived in several towns, and young Richard worked on Ohio River steamboats. Religion became important to him, and he joined the Methodist Episcopal (M.E.) faith when he was only 16 years old. Three years later, he was ordained and assigned to several churches in the Midwest.

Dissatisfied with the M.E. Church's segregated practices, Cain became attracted to the African Methodist Episcopal (A.M.E.) Church. The A.M.E. was organized by Blacks in 1787, in protest against segregated church services. In 1859, he was ordained a deacon. In 1860, wanting a more formal education, Cain enrolled in Wilberforce University. In 1861, he was assigned to a church in Brooklyn, New York.

After the Civil War ended in 1865, Cain was sent to South Carolina to help the newly freed slaves. Previously, the A.M.E. Church's growth had been limited by travel restrictions placed on free Blacks and slaves. With the restrictions removed, the church grew rapidly. Cain was instrumental in this growth and he organized churches throughout South Carolina.

Cain quickly saw that the time was right for Black political activism, so he attended the 1865 Colored Peoples Convention in Charleston. The next year, he became editor of the *South Carolina Ledger*, the first post-war Black newspaper in the state. The *Ledger* evolved into the *Missionary Record*, which lasted until 1872. In 1868, he was a delegate to the state's Constitutional Convention and was elected to the state senate.

Cain became known as "Daddy Cain" for his energy and enthusiasm on behalf of his fellow Blacks. This eventually jeopardized the safety of not only himself, but also his wife, Laura, and their family. After his election to the U.S. House of Representatives, the Cains complained of living in constant fear with their home guarded 24 hours a day.

Cain spoke on behalf of civil rights whenever possible, condemning ideas of colonizing Africa. Instead, he wanted equality and liberty for Blacks in the United States. He vehemently expressed his hopes for "no White, no Black ... but one common brotherhood, going forward in the progress of nations." Frequently, his no-nonsense common sense struck at the core of a problem. "We do not come here begging for our rights," he told fellow Congressmen. "We come here clothed in the garb of American citizenship. We come here demanding our rights in the name of justice."

To an accusation that only 1,800 Blacks had died in the Civil War, Cain pointed out that 37,000 Blacks were casualties in the Union Army alone. To those questioning the education level of Blacks, Cain retorted, "You robbed us for 200 years," and pointed out that slaves who sought education were severely punished.

Cain was re-elected in 1876 and seated in Congress when Reconstruction came to an end in 1877. He left South Carolina in early 1880, and became a bishop in Louisiana and Texas for the A.M.E. Church, which had grown to 400,000 members. While in Texas, Cain also became a founder and second president of Paul Quinn College in Waco.

In latter 1880, Richard H. Cain became Bishop for New York, New Jersey, New England, and Philadelphia until his death in 1887. Powerless to stop the wholesale disenfranchisements of southern Blacks politically, Cain used his religion to advance the rights of Blacks.

HENRY P. CHEATHAM
(1857 - 1935)

Following slavery, the progress made by Blacks in only thirty years of freedom was a story that Henry P. Cheatham wanted told. This former slave, who became a U.S. Congressman, asked his White colleagues in the U.S. House of Representatives for a federal grant to pay for a Black exhibit at the 1893 Columbia Exposition.

Henry P. Cheatham was born, in 1857, on a Henderson, North Carolina plantation. As the son of a house slave, his existence was less harsh than the lives of field slaves. The household environment enabled Henry to absorb a certain amount of culture and education. When he was only 8 years old, the Civil War ended, and he received his freedom. He then enrolled in school and pursued the education he realized was needed. In 1882, Cheatham received a bachelor's degree from Shaw University in Raleigh, North Carolina. With only an undergraduate degree, he was chosen to be principal of Normal School in Plymouth.

Cheatham married Louise Cherry, a music teacher at the school, and they subsequently had three children. Cheatham would later father three more children, by his second wife, Laura Joyner. Restless and yearning for more education and a different job, it was in 1887 that he received his graduate degree from Shaw and then began to study law.

While serving in public office, his leadership abilities became apparent. The Republican Party nominated him for Congress in 1888. When he won the election, Cheatham became the only Black in the House of Representatives. At the time, the elections of two other Blacks, Thomas E. Miller of South Carolina, and John Mercer Langston of Virginia, were initially contested and their subsequent appearance in Congress was delayed.

In the two terms that he served in Congress, Cheatham introduced 20 important bills. He asked for federal aid to set up and support schools so that all children, regardless of race or economic status, could get an education. He wanted the government to pay depositors who had lost money in the bankruptcy of the Freedmen's Bank. It was because of his Black pride, though, that he asked for the recognition of Black accomplishments at the World's Fair Exhibit in Chicago, but the request was buried in debate. Asked to introduce his own bill on the subject, Cheatham did, only to have the issue buried again. Not one to be discouraged and ever mindful of the importance of public opinion, Cheatham pushed for a report on the accomplishments of Colonial Blacks, and on the history of Black troops.

Although unsuccessful, Cheatham persevered in the belief that someone, someday, would listen. Nominated for the congressional race in 1894 and 1896, he lost both times to a White Democrat. In 1898, he lost the nomination to his brother-in-law, George H. White, who would be the last Black to serve in Congress for more than twenty years.

President William McKinley rewarded Cheatham for his political support by appointing him Recorder of Deeds for Washington, D.C. After this four-year assignment, he returned to North Carolina and launched another career that gave him tremendous satisfaction. In 1907, he became superintendent of a Black orphanage at Oxford. During his long tenure, until his death in 1935, he led a campus improvement and expansion program that replaced old wooden buildings with new brick structures. Cheatham also increased the orphanage's farm acreage and raised enough money to build two additional buildings.

At the time of Cheatham's death, almost 200 Black children had a home at the orphanage. His hopes for the orphanage came true, but his dreams for Black historical recognition would take much longer.

ROBERT C. DeLARGE
(1842 - 1874)

Robert C. DeLarge was one of the post-Civil War Blacks who labored to stop southern Whites from re-establishing political dominance after the Civil War. He and other Black men met at the Colored Peoples Convention, in November of 1865, to form a counter-strategy.

The Colored Peoples Convention petitioned Congress to throw "the strong arm of the law over the entire population of the state" and to give "equal suffrage" to all. Their combined efforts, with those of Blacks in other states, forced Congress to insist on the political equality, enjoyed however briefly, by Blacks during Reconstruction.

Born into slavery in Aiken, South Carolina, in 1842, DeLarge was a mulatto whose mother was of Haitian descent. He attended school in Charleston and received as much education as he could. The frustration with limited school opportunities for Blacks molded him into a vigorous fighter for public schools. His stand on public education was adopted at the 1867 Republican Party state convention, where De-Large served as chairman. This chairmanship influenced the convention to support popular elections and universal suffrage, land and tax reforms, an end to capital punishment, and funds for welfare, railroads and canals.

As a delegate to the state's Constitutional Convention of 1868, DeLarge's interest in land distribution to Blacks was evident. "There are 1,000 Freedman in this state who, within the last year, purchased land from the native Whites," De-Large told fellow delegates. "We propose that the government should aid us in the purchase of more lands, to be divided into small tracts and given on the above-mentioned credit to homeless families to cultivate for their support." He explained, "break up the large plantation system and turn more people into taxpayers."

Eventually, the convention asked Congress for an one million dollar grant to buy lands for resale to the state's poor. DeLarge explained, "I desire it to be distinctly understood that I do not advocate this measure simply for the benefit of my own race." Elected a member of the South Carolina legislature, DeLarge was appointment Land Commissioner for the state. In 1871, he reported that almost 2,000 small parcels of land had been or would be occupied by new homeowners. These homesteaders would be given eight years to pay for their land.

In 1870, DeLarge was elected to Congress by fewer than 1,000 votes over an independent Republican, Christopher Bowen, who later challenged the election. An investigation of the DeLarge-Bowen election revealed many accusations, including one that said DeLarge's legal counsel had been bribed by Bowen to withhold important evidence. In the end, the confusion of charges led the committee to declare that it could not figure out which of the two had been elected. The seat was declared vacant.

This stand-off, however, did not diminish DeLarge's popularity in South Carolina, where he owned a substantial amount of land. He subsequently would gain his admission to Congress, and hold his seat for two years. Throughout his term, DeLarge had to fight the continued challenge while also trying to make a meaningful contribution as a congressman.

One of his most important efforts was against the violence of the Ku Klux Klan, and he asked for federal protection for many of the Klan's targets. Eventually, federal troops were sent to South Carolina, and terrorist activity lessened. De Large and his family, which consisted of his wife and daughter, moved to Charleston, where he became a magistrate.

When he died of tuberculosis in 1874, DeLarge was only 31 years old. But his life story seemed that of a much older man because this former slave carried the fight for public education, land reform, and civil justice all the way to the nation's capital.

OSCAR S. DePRIEST
(1871 - 1951)

A prophecy was fulfilled when Oscar S. DePriest was elected to Congress in 1928. The prophet was George H. White, who left the United States Senate in 1901, vowing that his fellow Blacks would someday return to Congress.

The prediction by George White became a reality due to the large migration of Blacks to the North during and after World War I. DePriest became not only the first Black elected to Congress in the 20th Century, but also the first Black Congressman elected from the North.

DePriest was born in 1871 in a Florence, Alabama cabin to parents who were once slaves. His father, Alexander, was a farmer and teamster, and his mother, Mary, was a part-time laundress. In 1878, poverty and fear of lynching forced the family to move to Salina, Kansas, where Oscar attended grade school and took a two-year business course. At 17, he left home and lived meagerly for a year before settling in Chicago in 1889. He obtained work as a painter, advanced to a decorator, a contractor, and eventually, a real estate agent.

DePriest became very active in Chicago politics. After "paying his dues" at menial political jobs, DePriest got his reward. The Republican Party slated him as a candidate for Cook County Commissioner. DePriest was only 33 years old when he won his public office in 1904. He held the position of Cook County Commissioner until 1908. Later, DePriest set his sights on another goal, becoming the city's first Black alderman in 1915. Using his grassroots political experience, DePriest won the Republican nomination and defeated two White candidates in the election.

As a part of Mayor William (Big Bill) Thompson's political machine, DePriest acquired the power that patronage often brings. In 1928, he would become the first Black Congressman since Reconstruction. As a result, he was constantly in demand as a speaker. In taking these engagements, DePriest realized that he was a symbolic figure of the Negro in politics.

Meanwhile, DePriest had married and had a son, Oscar Jr. His wife, Jessie, was the object of controversy when she accepted an invitation from the President's wife, Mrs. Herbert Hoover. This incident typified White resentment over the first Black to sit in Congress since 1901. Although he realized his symbolic position in Congress, he was also realistic about what he could actually do to help his race. His success was limited by the fact that the nation was in the midst of the greatest economic depression of all time. The Depression was blamed for continued job discrimination in the South.

Some forms of discrimination, however, were more easily attacked; and DePriest did so. One example involved the refusal to serve Dr. Charles H. Wesley, of Howard University, in the dining room of the House of Representatives. An angry DePriest told a congressional committee: "I come from a group of people—and I am proud of it and make no apology for being a Negro—who have demonstrated their loyalty to the American government in every respect, making no exception.."

In 1934, DePriest lost his Congressional seat to another Black man, Arthur W. Mitchell. Mitchell was swept into office as a supporter of the Democratic President, Franklin D. Roosevelt. Following his defeat, DePriest returned to Chicago to resume his successful business interest. In 1943, he was re-elected to the Chicago City Council.

A kidney ailment caused DePriest's death in 1951. To the very end he had fought for racial equality in the job market. He also firmly believed that Black's goals could best be served by their involvement in practical politics. DePriest insisted to his dying day that he was of the "common herd."

ROBERT BROWN ELLIOTT
(1842 - 1884)

When Robert Brown Elliott entered the U.S. House of Representatives in 1871, the seat he took had symbolic significance. It was once occupied by a White congressman who was so enraged by a senator who advocated civil rights, that he physically beat him. Now the seat belonged to a Black man, who was judged by historians as "the ablest man in the legislature and South Carolina's most brilliant political organizer."

Some mystery surrounds Elliott's origins after his birth in 1842. It is reported that he was a British-born printer and sailor who came to the U.S. and Boston in 1867. The idea that he was Boston-born and educated in Britain may have been invented to give Elliott a U.S. citizenship. What is documented is that he was personable and intelligent, and that he worked as a typesetter in Boston, and was married in that city. The opportunity to be editor of a Black newspaper, the *South Carolina Ledger*, drew him to the state, just as the Reconstruction era was giving political power to the state's Black majority.

In 1868, Elliott was one of more than 100 delegates to the state's Constitutional Convention. While there, he vigorously opposed payment to former slave owners for their loss of free labor, and he fought against a poll tax requirement for voting. He championed compulsory education, which did not become a law in all states until 1918.

After serving in the state assembly, Elliott was appointed by the governor as Assistant Adjutant General of the state militia, where he worked to protect Blacks against the violence of the Ku Klux Klan. His crusades against the Klan, and against any favors for former Confederates, continued after his election to the U.S. House of Representatives in 1870.

In 1873, Elliott tried, but failed to be elected to the U.S. Senate, so he returned to the House in 1974. That year, he made a widely-acclaimed speech on behalf of Black civil rights. His speech came in support of a civil rights bill introduced by Sen. Charles Sumner, a White civil rights champion, who wanted to stop discrimination in education and public accommodations.

In reply to a former Confederate leader, Elliott said, in part, "...it is scarcely 12 years since that gentleman shocked the civilized world by announcing the birth of a government which rested on human slavery as its cornerstone. The progress of events has swept away that pseudo-government which rested on greed, pride and tyranny; and the race who he then ruthlessly spurned and trampled on are here to meet him in debate, and to demand that the rights which are enjoyed by their former oppressors—who vainly sought to overthrow a government which they could not prostitute to the base uses of slavery—shall be accorded to those who even in the darkness of slavery kept their allegiance true to freedom and the Union."

In 1874, Elliott, at the height of his political career, resigned from the U.S. Congress and returned to South Carolina's legislature determined to counteract criticism placed on the Black majority there. Later that year, Elliott was elected Speaker of the House. He and his wife, Grace, enjoyed a comfortable life in their South Carolina home.

In 1876, Elliott was elected State's Attorney General. However, the Attorney General post was taken from Elliott after the election of President Rutherford B. Hayes. Hayes, as part of an 1877 political compromise, returned power to southern Whites in certain states, including South Carolina. The Reconstruction Era of Black majority rule was over.

In 1881, Elliott moved to New Orleans, where he practiced law for almost three years until his death from malaria in 1884. Elliott was not yet 42 when he died. In fewer than 17 years in the United States, he made a historical mark on both state and national politics.

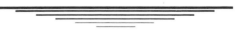

MIFFLIN W. GIBBS
(1823 - 1915)

The lure of gold and success drew Mifflin W. Gibbs to California and Canada. The need for an education led him to become a lawyer, judge, and a diplomat. Gibbs believed both goals, wealth and education were the keys to racial progress.

Gibbs was born in 1823, in Philadelphia to Jonathan Gibbs, a Wesleyan Methodist minister, and Maria Gibbs. His father's death, in 1831, left Mifflin and three other children to be reared by their invalid mother. Through an apprenticeship, Mifflin became a bootblack. But, young Gibbs was more interested in cultural things, so he joined with other Black men in a literary society called the Philomathean Institute. And although born free, he demonstrated his concern for enslaved Blacks by helping the Underground Railroad, an escape network for southern slaves.

It was in 1849, while on a speaking tour with that great Black leader Frederick Douglass, that the direction of Gibbs' life changed. He learned of the discovery of gold in California, and he became one of the 80,000 "Forty-niners" who rushed to California to make their fortune. After arriving in San Francisco, he opened a bootblack stand in front of the Union Hotel, and became part of the hustle and bustle of the booming city.

Later, he and a partner, Peter Lister, operated a shoe repair business. Optimistic and adventurous, Gibbs was a man of action; and he was active in the Black community, attending state conventions of Blacks in the 1850s, and founding a Black newspaper, *Mirror of the Times*, in 1855. His continued interest in race issues was evident in his sponsorship of a host of civil rights resolutions in the *Alto California*, the leading Black newspaper in the area.

Once again, the lure of gold and greater opportunity altered his life. In 1858, gold was discovered in British Columbia, Canada. This brought a rush of prospectors and businessmen, like Gibbs, from California to Canada. Gibbs made a quick fortune selling supplies to prospectors and buying real estate in the booming frontier town of Victoria, British Columbia.

In 1859, he briefly returned to the United States to marry Maria A. Alexander, with whom he would have five children. The coupled settled in Victoria, where Gibbs became active in the community, serving as a councilman from his district. Working as a contractor, he built a railroad, from the Queen Charlotte coal mines to Skidgate Harbor, and shipped the first cargo of coal mined on the Pacific coast to San Francisco.

In 1869, the restless and energetic Gibbs left Canada in pursuit of another goal, to finish his law education at Oberlin (Ohio) College, the school his wife had attended. The family then settled in Little Rock, Arkansas, a city considered by Gibbs to be receptive to Black ambition. He was admitted to the Arkansas State Bar in 1870, and elected City Judge in 1873. This prominence brought him to national attention and led to bigger political appointments; U.S. Land Office official in Little Rock, and U.S. Consul to Madagascar, the fourth largest island in the world, situated off the southeast coast of Africa.

Retiring from the government in 1901, Gibbs' many experiences put him in demand as a lecturer. Returning to Little Rock, he became a bank president and a partner in the local electric light company. He owned shares in several other companies and a substantial amount of Little Rock real estate. He also published his autobiography, *Shadow and Light*, before his death in 1915.

Ironically, although his life took many paths, Gibbs believed a skilled middle-class of Black farmers and industrial workers was essential for genuine racial progress.

■ ARCHIBALD HENRY GRIMKE ■
(1849 - 1930)

The name Grimke was in our history books long before Blacks were actually given their proper recognition in these very same books. Grimke was the name of two White abolitionist sisters, who were the first women to publicly speak out against slavery. Angelina and Sarah Moore Grimke had good reason to oppose slavery. They had three Black nephews born into slavery.

One of those nephews was Archibald Henry Grimke, born in 1849 to Henry Grimke, a white lawyer, and Nancy Weston, a slave, on a plantation near Charleston, South Carolina. The Grimkes were an exceptional southern family, and Henry admitted his fatherhood of Archibald, Francis and John. He sent them to a private school for free Blacks, and provided for their freedom in his 1852 will. This school was opened by Mayor Gilbert Pillsbury of Charleston and operated by his wife.

In 1867, with the help of Mrs. Pillsbury, Archibald and Francis were admitted to Lincoln University in Philadelphia. Both received bachelor's and master's degrees from Lincoln. Archibald, a religious young man and a Presbyterian Church elder at age 18, seemed destined to become a minister, but it was his brother Francis who would become a famous clergyman. Archibald decided to study law, and entered Harvard Law School in 1872. Sarah and Angelina had financially helped both Archibald and Francis through college. In 1874, Grimke became the second Black to earn a law degree from Harvard.

In 1879, Grimke opened up his law practice in Boston, struggling along with little business and poor clients. Often he would not receive payment for his services. He married Sarah Stanley and one year later their only child, Angelina Weld Grimke, was born. Unable to make a decent living as a Black lawyer, Grimke decided to try journalism. He founded and became editor of *The Hub*, in 1883, the first Black newspaper in the New England area. The newspaper was tied financially to the Republican Party and Henry Cabot Lodge, a

Harvard Law School graduate and member of a prominent Boston family.

Although the newspaper lasted only until 1886, Grimke and his new law partner, Butler R. Wilson, became highly successful lawyers. They were involved in a discrimination lawsuit that contributed to the enactment of a Massachusetts civil rights law in 1885. Grimke was now combining political involvement and civil rights campaigning. He was president of the Massachusetts Suffrage League, which fought discrimination and segregation. In 1884, he was Henry Cabot Lodge's alternate delegate to the Republican National Convention. Grimke's political experience led President Grover Cleveland to appoint him Consul to the Dominican Republic from 1894 to 1898. He was responsible for encouraging and protecting American interests, and was praised by the country's president.

Returning to the United States, Grimke focused his attention on civil rights, serving as president of the American Negro Academy from 1903 to 1916, and was an officer of the NAACP, receiving its Spingarn Medal in 1919. Grimke published many articles urging total equality for Blacks, and he wrote biographies on William Lloyd Garrison in 1891, Charles Sumner in 1892, and Denmark Vesey in 1901. In 1905, Archibald Grimke and his daughter moved into the Washington, D.C. home of his brother Francis. He was active with the NAACP until poor health forced his retirement in 1925.

When Grimke died in 1930, he left behind a distinguished life burdened with prevailing discrimination; beginning in slavery, through Reconstruction, and into segregation and prejudice. Grimke was, however, able to make a significant contribution and impact as a lawyer, editor, author, consul and civil rights leader.

BARBARA C. JORDAN
(1936 -   )

A drive for excellence led Barbara Jordan from the modest home of a Baptist minister to the influential corridors of Congress. Striving to meet the high expectations of her parents, she achieved the approval and respect of the American people.

Barbara Charline Jordan was born in 1936, in Houston, Texas, to Benjamin and Arlyne Jordan. To support his wife and three daughters, Benjamin Jordan added to his salary as a Baptist minister by working in a warehouse. While there was little money, there was always enough to eat and to keep a roof over their heads. And there was the parental insistence that the girls be good students.

The "A's" that Barbara brought home on her report cards pleased her as much as it did her parents. But, like many young people, she had not chosen a career path. Then, one day, fate introduced her to another Black female achiever, Edith Sampson, who was a lawyer and later became a judge. The occasion was a "Career Day" at Barbara's Houston high school, and Sampson was the guest speaker. Sampson provided a role model for Barbara, and she decided to become a lawyer.

In 1956, Jordan graduated *magna cum laude* from Texas Southern University in Houston, with a major in political science and history, and with a reputation as a winning debater. Three years later, after earning a law degree from Boston University, she returned to Houston to practice law. Her first office was her parent's dining room.

Almost immediately, Jordan got involved in politics, working for the 1960 Presidential campaign of John F. Kennedy. Twice, in 1962 and 1964, she lost elections to the State House of Representatives. Learning from her mistakes and undaunted by those losses, she won election to the State Senate in 1966, the first Black woman to do so from the state of

Texas. In 1968, she was re-elected to a four-year term. In the Senate, her abilities soon became evident, and she was chosen as the outstanding freshman senator during her first year. Among the many bills bearing her staunch support were those improving minimum wage, workmen's compensation, and the Texas Fair Employment Practices.

In 1972, Jordan moved onto the national scene, winning election to the U.S. House of Representatives, and becoming the first Black congresswoman from the Deep South. Jordan was appointed to the House Judiciary Committee. The Watergate scandal was reaching its height, and the Judiciary Committee was a major force in the drama. As a Committee member, Jordan became nationally known and was among the first of those who signed impeachment articles against President Richard M. Nixon in 1974. Her keen intellect, as demonstrated in the media during the Watergate Hearings, made her a sought-after speaker for the Democratic Party and many groups.

In her role as lawmaker, she was a consistent force on behalf of ordinary Americans. Jordan worked for increased school aid, expanded voting rights, subsidies to urban mass transit, and grants to metropolitan police departments. She wanted free legal services for the poor, and the extension of Social Security benefits to housewives. She voted against the Alaskan pipeline because of environmental concerns, and she called for limits on oil company profits. Jordan focused on bread-and-butter issues of everyday living.

Once, when asked why she never married, Jordan explained that her job was too time-consuming to give marriage the effort that it required. After leaving Congress, Jordan turned her dedication to teaching at the University of Texas, where she became the kind of role model that she once admired.

JOHN R. LYNCH
(1847 - 1939)

At least twice, circumstances conspired to deny the rightful status of John R. Lynch. The first occurred when his father's death ended the family's chance to leave slavery. The second came in 1877, when Lynch was denied a third term in Congress. His years in between tell the story of a man who, craving education and justice, was denied formal training and fairness. It is also the story of a man who overcame his obstacles.

Lynch's father, Patrick, an immigrant from Ireland, was a planter near Vidalia, Louisiana. His mother, Catherine White, was a slave. After Lynch's birth in 1847, his father planned to move the family to New Orleans and free them. His father's fatal illness ended this plan. A friend, promising to free the family, took title of the Lynchs from Patrick. However, the promise was not kept, and the family was sold to a planter in Natchez, Mississippi. Lynch was freed in 1863, when the Union Army took control of the city.

After the Civil War ended in 1865, Lynch learned the photography trade and managed a successful business in Natchez. Although the total of his formal education was only four months in night school, he educated himself by reading books and newspapers, and by secretly eavesdropping on class lessons in a White school. His determination combined with natural abilities made him a fluent and effective speaker and writer.

Lynch took advantage of the post-war political opportunities for Blacks, becoming first a Justice of the Peace, and then a Mississippi State Representative. In his service to the state, he was particularly proud of the new public school system that established schools for Black children. He was only 26 years old, when he was elected to Congress. There, he continued to be an activist, introducing many bills and arguing on their behalf. Perhaps his greatest effort was in the long debate on the 1875 *Civil Rights Act* that banned discrimination in public accommodations (This Act was later overturned by the United States Supreme Court).

The contesting of Lynch's third term election, in 1876, was typical of the political upheaval of the times. He was not allowed to take his seat, but he ran again in 1880. This election was also contested, and Lynch battled for a year before being seated. At this point, the next election was almost upon him, leaving him little time to campaign. He lost the 1882 election by only 600 votes.

It wasn't until 1884 that Lynch took time to get married. He and his wife, the former Ella Sommerville, had a daughter before their divorce. During the Spanish-American War of 1898, he was appointed Treasury Auditor, and then Paymaster. In 1901, he began serving with the Regular Army, in tours of duty in the United States, Cuba, and the Philippines. During this time, he sold his Mississippi real estate holdings of 1,700 acres.

After retiring from the Army in 1911, Lynch married Cora Williams; and they moved to Chicago, where he practiced law and once again became involved in real estate. After his death in 1939, he was buried with military honors in Arlington National Cemetery.

Lynch left behind many examples of his eloquence, such as this excerpt from his speech on Black patriotism: "They were faithful and true to you then; they are no less so today. And yet they ask no special favors as a class; they ask no special protection as a race. They feel that they purchased their inheritance, when upon the battlefields of this country, they watered the tree of liberty with the precious blood that flowed from their loyal veins. They ask no favors, they desire—and must have—an equal chance in the race of life."

GEORGE WASHINGTON MURRAY
(1853 - 1926)

After the Civil War, one of the Black orphans who had to look after himself was George Washington Murray. It did not appear likely that this friendless waif would ever amount to anything.

Murry was born, in 1853, to slave parents in Sumter County, South Carolina. He was intelligent and somehow managed to acquire ample education which enabled him to teach. Later in life, he would often relate to the fact that he had never been in a school, until he went there as a teacher.

Murray, however, was not uneducated when he was elected to Congress in the 1890s. He was almost 40 years old, and by that time had attended South Carolina University and the State Normal Institute. He was admitted into the university at age 21, by taking a competency test. His studies ended abruptly two years later, when the University was once again closed to Black students. Rather than becoming discouraged, Murray channeled his energies into other directions. For more than 10 years, he taught school, purchased enough acreage of land to farm, attended the State Normal Institute as a part-time student, and entered Republican Party politics.

In 1890, President Benjamin Harrison appointed Murray as Customs Inspector for the Port of Charleston. That same year, Murray tried but lost the party's nomination for election to Congress. Determined, he attempted again in 1892, this time winning by only 40 votes. Murray tried in vain to stop the disenfranchisement of his fellow Blacks. The Presidency and both Houses of Congress were now controlled by Democrats, who were determined to repeal certain human rights. Trying to accomplish what he could, Murray campaigned for trade schools to teach skills, and for aid to the poor and aged. After being elected to a second term in 1895, he spent his efforts trying to combat political fraud and harassment in South Carolina.

In addition to his struggles in Congress, Murray took on the responsibilities of a family, marrying and eventually fathering two children. He bought 10,000 acres of land in South Carolina and sold parcels to other Blacks. He added to his accomplishments by inventing and patenting various farm implements, including a fertilizer, planter, and harvester.

With the Democrats firmly in control, the Republicans were split into opposing factions. Efforts to secure the rights of Blacks were abandoned. Murray's reactions are quoted in the book *Black Americans in Congress*, "We stand helpless and amazed. I declare that the patient, long-suffering, generous Black man has never attempted to domineer anywhere in the country. At the very dawn of freedom, when the refusal to act on the part of the master class placed the reins of government in his hands with only a handful of White men in his party, he gave nearly every position of honor and emolument to them..."

In 1905, Murray moved to Chicago, where he wrote and privately published two books, *Race Ideals* in 1914, and *Light in Dark Places* in 1925. He continued to lecture about his experiences in his rise from orphan to congressman. In the spring of 1926, he became ill, having waited too long to obtain a much-needed surgical operation.

In April, he died, leaving behind his wife, Cornelia, and two children. The funeral service for this last Black congressman from South Carolina included a eulogy which highlighted Murray's independence of thought on behalf of Blacks during the Reconstruction period. This eulogy was presented by a fellow freedom-fighter, John R. Lynch, another significant Black congressman who had witnessed the rise and fall of Black rights during Reconstruction.

■ PINCKNEY BENTON STEWART PINCHBACK ■
(1837-1921)

As a businessman, Pinckney B. S. Pinchback was proud and successful. As a Black, he was a frustrated patriot who spent much of his life beating at the wall of racial injustice.

Pinchback was born in 1837, the son of a White Mississippi planter, William Pinchback, and Eliza Stewart, whose ancestry was Black, White, and Indian. William had emancipated Eliza before Pinckney's birth, so the boy was born free. When he was about 10 years-old, Pinckney and his older brother, Napoleon, were sent to school in Cincinnati.

Soon, Eliza and her eight other children joined them to avoid re-enslavement after William's death. Denied any part of the Pinchback inheritance, the family was poor. Young Pinckney got a job as a cabin boy on the ships that navigated the lakes and rivers of the South and the Midwest. After working hard to become a ship steward, his hopes for better jobs were met with reminders that his race prevented further advancement.

In 1860, Pinchback married Nina Hawthorne, and they would later have six children. In 1862, he went to New Orleans, where he enlisted in the Union Army to fight in the Civil War. He was assigned to recruit Black volunteers, and he organized two regiments. Pinchback later resigned as captain of the first regiment because of racial discrimination against his troops. After recruiting a second regiment, he resigned in disgust because he was not permitted to lead it. Pinchback argued his troops "did not ask for social equality and did not expect it, but they demanded political rights-they wanted to be men."

Disillusioned, Pinchback moved to Louisiana, where he became involved in politics, as a founder of the state's Republican Party. His eloquence, intelligence, and leadership abilities were at last given a chance to blossom. In 1867, as a Louisiana Constitutional Convention delegate, he worked for universal suffrage, civil rights guarantees, and free schools. The following year, he was elected to the state senate, eventually becoming president pro tem of that body. He succeeded to the post of lieutenant governor after the death of the incumbent. Briefly, from Dec. 9, 1872 to Jan. 13, 1873, he was the state's acting Governor during the impeachment proceedings against that incumbent, Henry Clay Warmoth.

In 1872, Pinchback had been elected congressman-at-large on the Republican ticket, but his seat was contested and finally won by a Democratic Party opponent. He was then elected to a six-year term as a U.S. Senator, but this seat, too, was challenged and finally denied him after a three-year battle.

Elegant in dress and aristocratic in conduct, Pinchback was an astute politician. For example, he traded his support in political elections for assurances of Black civil rights. In 1882, Pinchback received an important appointment, Customs Inspector for the Port of New Orleans. He regulated the merchandise and the passengers going into and out of this busy port until 1885.

During his political career, Pinchback had various business interests, including a partnership in the Mississippi River Packet Company. His business success enabled him to live on his prosperous investments. From 1892 to 1895, he returned to the national scene as U.S. Marshal in New York City.

Pinchback continued to exercise his political influence for two more decades until his death in 1921. Disinherited in his youth and disillusioned by racial prejudice, Pinchback harnessed his abilities as a leader and intellectual to become a success both in business and in governmental service.

■■■ ADAM CLAYTON POWELL, JR. ■■■
(1908-1972)

Powell was a rebel with a cause, a self-described radical and fighter. A militant who used boycotts and pickets long before they became fashionable. These descriptions portray, in part, Adam Clayton Powell Jr., the first Black congressman from New York. This unconventional man left his mark on a large number of labor and education reforms.

Powell was born in New Haven, Connecticut, in 1908, the same year his father, Adam Clayton Powell Sr., became pastor of the famous Abyssinian Baptist Church, in the district of New York. The family also consisted of Powell's mother, Mattie, and older sister, Blanche. They lived an upper middle-class life with the senior Powell's clergyman salary augmented by sizeable Harlem real estate holdings. Powell was a good student and was graduated from Colgate University in Hamilton, New York, in 1930.

After graduation, the younger Powell became an assistant pastor for his father. He soon began to demonstrate the leadership ability displayed throughout his life. In 1931, the St. Louis Urban League began a Jobs-for-Negroes drive in which a chain store was boycotted because it refused to employ Black workers. Powell became the leader of a series of such boycotts.

Powell also led several thousand protestors to City Hall demanding a reversal of the firing of Black doctors from the Harlem Hospital. In 1937, at age 28, he succeeded his retiring father as minister of the church, with a congregation of 10,000. The church was the scene of the 1940 rally, leading to a successful bus boycott that resulted in the hiring of Black bus drivers and mechanics.

Capitalizing on his gaining popularity, Powell campaigned and won a city council seat in 1941, thereby becoming New York's first Black councilman. By attacking the White political machine and capitalizing on his nonpartisan independence, Powell succeeded in creating a large political machine of his own. His wide-ranging interests and opinions brought him national attention, as he spoke out against discrimination.

In 1944, Powell was elected to Congress. Democrats, Republicans, Socialists, and Communists sought his favor. When he sided with the majority Democratic Party, he was repaid with an appointment on the House Education and Labor Committee, for which he became chairman in 1961. Under his five year leadership, 60 pieces of legislation involving billions of dollars for anti-poverty measures were passed. Using a political base of Blacks and other ethnic groups, Powell spent 26 years in Congress fighting racial bias on all fronts. Much of what he fought for was contained in the omnibus *Civil Rights Act* of 1964, signed by President Lyndon B. Johnson.

Falsely charged with misusing public funds, Powell was refused his congressional seat in 1967. Attributing racism, he fought this decision all the way to the Supreme Court, which ruled, in 1969, that his removal from Congress was unconstitutional. Although he regained his seat that year, he was defeated in the Democratic primary in 1970, by attorney Charles B. Rangel.

In 1933, Powell married Isabel Washington, a dancer, and he adopted her son. After the marriage ended in divorce, he married Hazel Scott, a singer and pianist, in 1945. Their only child, Adam Clayton Powell III (Skipper), was born a year later. This marriage also ended in divorce in 1960, after which Powell married Yvette Flores Diago.

Hospitalized late in 1969, Powell underwent tests that diagnosed cancer. He died in 1972, at the age of 63. Thousands of mourners paid their respects as his body laid in state in the Abyssinian Baptist Church. They grieved for the loss of a man who was a symbol of Black protest as well as Black power and achievement. He was a leader who defined Black Power as "a dynamic process of continuous change toward a society of true equals."

JOSEPH HAYNE RAINEY
(1832-1887)

The Ku Klux Klan, the secret society of White terrorists, was founded in 1866. Its aim was the restoration of White supremacy in the southern states. In 1871, a federal law was passed to curb the Klan's activities. The enforcement of that law was a prime goal of Joseph Hayne Rainey, the first Black seated in the U.S. House of Representatives and the first to preside over that House.

When it came to the Klan, Rainey's home state of South Carolina was safer than most. Rainey was in the forefront of all important discussions about Klan violence in the South. Federal troops occupied regions of South Carolina, capturing many Klan leaders and forcing hundreds of Klansmen to flee. By 1872, the violence had greatly decreased and the Reconstruction era of the Klan was ended.

Rainey's parents, Edward and Gracey, were slaves when their son was born, in 1832, in Georgetown, South Carolina. While the boy was still young, his father's barbering business was so successful that the elder Rainey was able to purchase the family's freedom. During a brief stay in Philadelphia, in 1859, Rainey met and married Susan, who returned with him to South Carolina. Like his father, Rainey became a barber.

After the Civil War broke out in 1861, the Confederacy drafted Rainey to work on the military fortifications at Charleston's harbor. Working there on the coast, Rainey dreamed of escaping from the military drudgery to a life without the stigma of color. The dream became reality when he and his wife boarded a ship bound for the West Indies. Rainey worked as a barber in Bermuda and his wife worked as a dressmaker. He studied the manners and conversation of his educated customers. Hearing that opportunities for Blacks were better in postwar South Carolina, the Raineys returned home.

Entering politics during the Reconstruction era, Rainey was elected to the State House and Senate. In 1870, he was elected to the U.S. House of Representatives, becoming the first Black to be seated. While Rainey was fighting for civil rights legislation, he was often confronted with racial discrimination. Treated somewhat fairly in Washington, he talked of his humiliation in other areas. Such insults as being denied first-class traveling accommodations, or being forced to eat with servants added to his mental anguish.

While pleading for fairness, Rainey pointed out that the newly freed Black majority in southern states did not take political advantage of the White minority. Black historian Carter Woodson quoted Rainey as saying, "Our (state) convention which met in 1868, and in which Negroes were in a large majority, did not pass any proscriptive or disfranchising acts, but adopted a liberal constitution, securing alike equal rights to all citizens, White and Black, male and female, as far as possible."

It was in May of 1874 that Rainey achieved another Black American first. When the House speaker was absent, Rainey presided over that session. After failing to win re-election in 1878, Rainey was appointed Special Agent for the Treasury Department in South Carolina. After two years, he left this position and turned to a business career, opening a banking and brokerage firm in Washington. When that failed, he became a partner in a successful wood and coal business.

When Rainey's health began failing, the family moved to Georgetown, South Carolina where his wife operated a millinery shop. Only 55 years old when he died in 1887, Rainey was survived by five children. He lived his life not only as a trailblazer, but also as a noble warrior in a battle against overwhelming odds.

JAMES T. RAPIER
(1837-1883)

The disillusionment and pain suffered by the Black congressmen of the Reconstruction era was best explained by James T. Rapier, the Black congressmen from Alabama.

Pointing out that he was a "peer of the proudest" while sitting in Congress, he complained that he was "not equal to the most degraded" while traveling to and from Alabama. He talked of "legislating for a free people" while his own "chains of civil slavery" hung about him. Rapier said no inn between Washington and Montgomery, Alabama, would give him a bed or a meal. That any White, even a criminal, would be better treated than he, a congressman on his trips to and from the capital.

Rapier's comments were made before the House of Representatives, in 1875, in support of a civil rights bill which Congress was debating. The bill, which began as a strong provision for Black rights, finally passed in a watered-down version. Even that law, however, was later struck down by the U.S. Supreme Court.

Rapier's mother was a free Black, named Susan. Disagreement occurs about his father, who was either a White plantation owner or a free Black barber. James Rapier was born in 1837, and was able to get an education, by moving to Canada where he attended several schools. He also studied at the University of Glasgow in Scotland. The result, according to Black leader W.E.B. DuBois, was a person "well-educated" and a "man of power."

During the Civil War, Rapier returned to the United States and settled in Tennessee, where he taught school. He was a correspondent for a Northern newspaper when the Union army seized Nashville. His law studies enabled him to be admitted to the bar. Although only a few short years in Tennessee, he was the keynote speaker at the Tennessee Negro Suffrage Convention and a delegate to the State Constitution Convention in 1865.

With the Civil War over, Rapier returned home. A life-long bachelor, Rapier devoted his time to becoming a successful cotton farmer, until the political climate in Alabama gave him a chance to participate in the political process. Rapier went to the Alabama State House to help write a constitution. He helped establish the state's Republican Party and served as its Vice President. His influence was such that he became a target of the Ku Klux Klan.

In 1968, fearing violence, Rapier fled from his home in Florence, Alabama, and remained hidden in Montgomery, Alabama, for almost one year. Two years later, no longer fearing for his life, he became the Republican candidate for Secretary of State, but lost the election to a White man. In 1871, he received a party patronage assignment as Internal Revenue Assessor for the Montgomery district, a job he held for two years.

In addition to politics, Rapier was involved in the labor movement as an organizer for the Colored National Labor Union. In 1870, he was elected vice president of the National Negro Labor Union and became president of the Alabama Negro Labor Union. He also found time to establish, publish, and edit a newspaper for Blacks, the *Montgomery Sentinel.*

Eventually, Rapier returned to politics, convinced that activity was the only hope for Blacks. In 1872, he campaigned and won a seat in Congress, defeating a former Confederate officer. Rapier worked on the education and labor committee, using his abilities to support civil rights for Blacks. Defeated for a second term because of White return to power, he once again turned to farming.

From 1877 until his death in 1883 of tuberculosis, he was an Internal Revenue Collector; and in this, too, his performance and professionalism was rated "excellent."

ROBERT SMALLS
(1839 - 1915)

In Charleston, South Carolina, the Confederate officers of the ship Planter had gone ashore to enjoy themselves. Meanwhile, in the harbor, their ship was being hijacked by an ingenuous, 23-year-old Black man, a crew member, with a daring idea for escape to the North.

With his wife and two children smuggled aboard, along with other civilians, Robert Smalls sailed the *Planter* out of Confederate waters and delivered it to the Union forces. The ship was worth more than $60,000 and Smalls was hailed a hero.

A Union officer wrote, "This man Robert Smalls is superior to any who have come into our lines—intelligent as many of them have been." As a reward, Smalls received $1,500 and was appointed a pilot of ships in the U.S. Navy. Later, when the *Planter's* captain panicked under fire, Smalls took the helm again. For this, he was promoted to Captain and later advanced to Commander.

Smalls was born in 1839, in Beaufort, South Carolina, to Lydia Smalls, a house slave of the McKee family. At his mother's suggestion, Smalls was taken by his master to Charleston, in 1851, to be hired out for wages. She feared his nature was too rebellious for plantation living. With most of his wages going to the McKee's, Smalls worked as a waiter, lamplighter and horse driver.

Eventually, Smalls became a rigger and learned the skills of a seaman. When he was almost 18, he married Hannah Jones, a hotel maid. She would bear him two daughters, Elizabeth and Sarah, and a son, Robert, who died of smallpox at age three.

After the Civil War, Smalls returned to Beaufort and bought the house where he and his mother had been slaves. He then began a political career that saw him elected first as a State Representative in 1868, and then as a State Senator.

In 1875, Smalls was elected to Congress from South Carolina and served until 1887. While he was successful in obtaining projects that benefitted his state, he was frequently harassed by southern Democrats trying to reclaim South Carolina from the Black Republicans. Smalls was a generous and forgiving man. He was, for example, kind to his former masters, the McKees. After they lost everything in the war, they were given a house and farm acreage by Smalls. Later, he tried to get jobs in Washington for the McKee children.

In 1878, Smalls lost his Congressional seat because of voter harassment and cheating, and his 1880 election was not confirmed until the end of the term. When he lost his bid in the 1886 election, Smalls tried and failed to prove that the election was fraudulent. His thoughts of running again, in 1888, were discouraged by former supporters who wanted a younger candidate.

After Hannah Smalls died in 1883, Smalls remained a widower until 1890, when he married Annie Wigg, a teacher. From that union came a son, William Robert, born in 1892. In 1895, Smalls was one of six Blacks at the State's Constitutional Convention. Despite his efforts, southern Whites regained power and once again took political power from Blacks.

Robert Smalls was able, before his death in 1915, to save the lives of two Blacks jailed, in Beaufort, who were threatened with lynching. The boy who was too rebellious to be a slave grew up to be a war-time hero and a champion of his people in Congress.

JAMES MONROE TROTTER
(1842 - 1892)

James Monroe Trotter was an army officer, author and holder of the highest federal job open to Blacks. Yet even more significant than any of these achievements was the fact that he was a life-long hero to his son, William Monroe Trotter, who made his own mark as a militant civil rights leader.

James was born in 1842, in Grand Gulf, Mississippi, one of three children of Richard Trotter and his slave, Letitia. In 1854, Letitia was sent with her son and two daughters to live in the free city of Cincinnati. James found work on the Ohio river boats as a cabin boy and bellboy. He attended a school for freed slaves in Cincinnati, and other Ohio schools at Athens and Hamilton. He was, however, primarily self-taught, which was no small task amid the hurdles of earning a living, while many jobs were closed to him because of race.

At the outbreak of the Civil War in 1861, Trotter was teaching school in southwestern Ohio. Believing the war to be a battle against slavery, he enlisted in a Black army unit. This unit was commanded primarily by Whites. But, Trotter was an outstanding recruit, earning promotion through the ranks to second lieutenant, one of the four Black officers in the regiment. In 1864, as the Union forces fought through the Carolinas toward Virginia, Trotter was wounded, but fought on until the war was over in 1865.

Trotter was unyielding when confronted with unfairness. Blatant and unreasonable discrimination was something he could not tolerate. He was, for example, a leader in the successful struggle to lift the wages of Black troops from the $10 monthly laborer's pay to the $13 paid to White soldiers. When the war ended, Trotter was rewarded for his military service with a job in the Boston post office.

Three years later, in 1868, he married an old friend, Virginia Isaacs of Chilicothe, Ohio. The Trotters, who had taught together in pre-war years, would become the parents of William Monroe, Maude, and Bessie. The family was comfortable, living in a predominantly White Boston suburb.

Trotter was a proud man, and he wanted his fellow Blacks to live up to their full-potential and get the recognition they deserved. Nowhere is this more evident than in his 1878 music book, *Music and Some Highly Musical People,* published in Boston and New York. In the book, Trotter pointed with pride at Black achievements in music and hoped other Blacks would share this pride. But, he also urged Whites to read the book and take note of the Black accomplishments.

In 1882, Trotter once again took a stand against the White establishment. He resigned his post office job because a White man was promoted over him. He carried the protest even further by leaving the Republican Party, which controlled the federal bureaucracy, and joined the Democratic Party. Here, too, he gained a leadership position among Black democrats and was given a coveted political appointment by President Grover Cleveland.

In 1887, Trotter became Recorder of Deeds in Washington, D.C., the highest federal post open to Blacks other than a diplomatic assignment. This job was also a money-maker because a real estate boom generated a large number of commissions for Trotter. When the Republicans won the 1888 presidential election and took over federal patronage jobs, Trotter returned to Boston and entered real estate.

In 1892, he died of tuberculosis, leaving his wife and three children. His only son, William Monroe, would become the first Black elected to Phi Beta Kappa in his junior year at Harvard University. Many years later, William told an interviewer about the greatest influence and inspiration in his life—his father, James Monroe Trotter.

JAMES MILTON TURNER
(1840 - 1915)

In 19th Century United States, some Americans, both Black and White, favored Blacks going to Africa to establish colonies. Some Blacks did in fact go, and they founded the country of Liberia, a nation about the size of Ohio on the west coast of Africa. When he was only 31 years old, James Milton Turner was appointed U.S. Minister-Resident and Consul-General to Liberia by President Ulysses S. Grant.

Turner was born a slave in 1840, in St. Louis County, Missouri. When he was 4, he and his mother, Hannah, were purchased from slavery by his father, John Turner, who paid $50 for the family. James was taught to read by Catholic nuns, who secretly operated a school for slaves in a cathedral. Later, he attended classes in the basement of a Baptist church. When he was 14, he enrolled in the high school classes offered by Oberlin College, in Ohio.

In the Civil War, he served as a Union officer's valet. A life-long limp reportedly came from a war wound received at the battle of Shiloh, where thousands of Union and Confederate troops were killed in 1862. After the war, Turner returned to Missouri and became a dedicated fighter for the establishment of Black schools. As a result, the Kansas City school board appointed Turner a teacher in the state's first tax-supported Black school in Boonville, Missouri.

Turner can also take the credit for the establishment of Lincoln Institute, now Lincoln University, at Jefferson City, Missouri. He personally raised money from Black soldiers and successfully prodded the state legislature to appropriate money for the Institute. Turner became not only a Lincoln board member, but also the state's Assistant Superintendent of Schools in charge of establishing free Black public schools.

His leadership and reputation drew him into the politics of the Reconstruction era, and it was his support of Grant that won him the diplomatic post to Liberia in 1871. Turner's experiences in Africa triggered his opposition to Black American colonization. The uprising of the various tribes and the instability of the Liberian government were the reasons for his opposition, along with the hot climate. Instead of Blacks moving to Africa, he urged Americans to send aid to improve the conditions of Africans. After seven years in Liberia, Turner returned to the United States in 1878, and married Ella de Burton.

Turner became involved in the Black migration from the South to the Plain States. This migration, called the "Great Exodus," centered on Kansas; and Turner set up a way-station in St. Louis for migrating Blacks. He was also involved in a proposal for 160 acres for each Black settling in Oklahoma.

Turner also embraced the cause of the Black members of the Cherokee Indian Nation, who had not received their portion of a congressional grant for property taken from them. In 1886, he urged President Grover Cleveland to pressure Congress into paying the Black Indians. This effort was successful three years later, when $75,000 was appropriated by Congress for the freed Blacks in the Cherokee, Shawnee and Delaware tribes.

An accident took Turner's life in 1915. He was killed by a railroad car explosion in Ardmore, Oklahoma. His body was taken back to St. Louis, where once the city's Blacks had paraded in joy at Turner's successful return from Liberia. They now would honor him with the city's largest Black funeral.

Turner was praised much the same as he had once praised Dred Scott, the Black slave who ignited a major U.S. Supreme Court debate that moved the country toward civil war. Scott, he had said, "deserved a prominent place in Missouri's history." No Missourian, however, had done more for his people than Turner.

ROBERT C. WEAVER
(1907 -)

Fulfilling his mother's (Florence) expectations, Robert C. Weaver became the most important Black in the federal government, heading up many governmental agencies.

Florence Freeman Weaver admired intellectual and cultural achievement, and was herself possessed of both culture and intellect. Her father was a Harvard graduate and the first Black American to earn a doctorate in dentistry. She and her husband, Mortimer, a postal clerk, provided a middle-class home life for Robert and his brother. The family lived in a Washington, D.C. suburb with fewer than ten Black families.

Robert was born in Washington, in 1907, and discovered discrimination when he and his brother had to travel to a Black school rather than attend a nearby school for Whites. By the time he was a senior in high school, he was a self-employed electrician, but his mother had other aspirations for him. So Robert enrolled in Harvard, where he earned a bachelor's degree, *cum laude*, in 1929, a master's degree in 1931, and a doctorate's degree in 1934.

In the 1930s, the nation was in the midst of its greatest economic depression, and Weaver's degrees were in economics. President Franklin D. Roosevelt and his wife, Eleanor, were sensitive to the special needs of Blacks, and Weaver found himself in demand as a federal government adviser on minority problems. His long government career began in 1933, as an advisor to Secretary of the Interior Harold Ickes. During his four years in that job, Weaver married Ella V. Haith, and they adopted a son, Robert Jr.

In the next decade, Weaver had so many government jobs that he became a very important force in securing rights for Blacks. He was part of Roosevelt's "Black Cabinet," which integrated federal agencies, provided low-rent housing and jobs, and made sure Blacks were involved in the Depression's government-sponsored projects.

After the Depression and World War II, Weaver worked for several philanthropic foundations and served the state of New York as a specialist in housing. His expertise in housing increased after he was appointed Vice Chairman of the New York City Housing and Redevelopment Board in 1959. Weaver's interest in housing rose from a conviction that segregated housing was the primary cause of segregated schools and racial separation in other areas.

Weaver was one of the first to recognize the effects of federal slum clearance projects on Black city-dwellers. He criticized the removal of Blacks from prime locations in the city to other potential slum sites. He also protested the higher rents in renewal projects that excluded Blacks from the neighborhoods where they once lived.

Weaver's abilities got national recognition in 1960, when President-elect John F. Kennedy named him administrator of the Housing and Home Finance Agency. This was the highest federal administrative position ever given to a Black, and it carried the responsibility of more than $300 million in federal spending. One year later, an even greater distinction came to Weaver. Named Secretary of Housing and Urban Development, he became was the first Black ever to serve in a Presidential cabinet. Later, Weaver turned his attention to college teaching and consulting assignments.

Weaver is the recipient of many awards and honorary degrees, and author of several books, including *Negro Labor: A National Problem, The Negro Ghetto, The Urban Complex, Dilemmas of Urban America.* In 1962, Weaver received the NAACP Spingarn Medal.

For decades, Weaver worked within the government for civil rights. Although believing the best way to racial equality was to fight hard but legally, he applauded the 1960's sit-in demonstrations as "courageous and effective." The inspiration given him by his mother to be the best that he could be, he has passed on to many others.

GEORGE M. WHITE
(1852 - 1918)

As a Black man, George H. White had seen the whole discouraging story: the Black rise to political power after the Civil War; the loss of that power to southern Whites; and the birth of Jim Crow. As the last Black Congressman of the post-Reconstruction era, White left Congress in 1901 with the below parting words to his White colleagues:

"You may tie us and then taunt us for a lack of bravery, but one day we will break the bonds. You may use our labor for two and a half centuries and then taunt us for our poverty, but let me remind you, we will not always remain poor. You may withhold even the knowledge of how to read God's word and learn the way of the earth to glory and then taunt us for our ignorance, but we would remind you that there is plenty of room at the top, and we are climbing... This, Mr. Chairman, is perhaps the Negroes' temporary farewell to the American Congress; but let me say, Phoenix-like, he will rise up some day and come again. These parting words are in behalf of an outraged, heartbroken, bruised and bleeding, but God-fearing people, faithful, industrious, loyal people—full of potential force..."

White was born in 1852, in Rosindale, North Carolina, to a family that farmed and made barrels. Little else is known about his family except that his parentage was a mixture of Black, White, and Indian. Somehow, he managed to obtain schooling while working to save money for college. By age 21, he was able to enter Howard University and worked his way through school by teaching in the summers. White had his sights set on a law career and he studied law while he taught school. After passing the state bar examination, he opened a law office in New Bern, North Carolina in 1879.

White's political ambitions took him to the State House and State Senate. Ironically, when he decided to run for Congress, his rival was his brother-in-law, Henry Cheatham. Both men were married to daughters of Henry Cherry, a

State Assemblyman. Cheatham won in 1894, but two years later, both Black and White voters elected White to the U.S. House of Representatives. He was re-elected in 1898, despite a wicked, name-calling campaign.

White argued tirelessly for equal constitutional rights. Time and time again, he told White congressmen about the persistent denial of equal access to opportunity. Even in his final House speech, White lectured colleagues on how to treat the "Negro problem": "Treat him as a man; go into his home and learn of his social conditions; learn of his cares, his troubles, and his hopes for the future; gain his confidence; open the doors of industry to him... Measure the standard of his race by its best material, cease to mould prejudicial and unjustified public sentiment against him..."

Two years before leaving Congress in 1901, White and some business associates purchased 1,700 acres in New Jersey, to establish an all-Black town. Whitesboro grew to a community of more than 80 by 1906. However, White moved to Philadelphia in 1905, where he established a bank and conducted a successful law practice in the heart of the Black business district. He was also active in community affairs, becoming an officer of the local NAACP branch.

After several years in ill health, White died in 1918. He had lived to see Whitesboro offer single-family homes to Blacks who farmed, fished, and worked in a sawmill. Each family bought their home and farm on easy-payment terms arranged by White. The farm boy who had worked to pay for his education became a national spokesman for his race, whose deeds also benefitted hundreds of Black families.

RICHARD R. WRIGHT, SR.
(1855? - 1947)

One morning in 1868, in Atlanta, Georgia's Storrs Church Sunday School, the children were eagerly awaiting a visitor. His name was Gen. Oliver Otis Howard, head of the Freedmen's Bureau and the man for whom Howard University would be named.

During the visit, Howard asked the students what he should tell the children up North about them. "Tell them, general, we're rising," answered one boy. That boy was Richard R. Wright, Sr.; and the incident inspired a poem, *Howard at Atlanta*, by the famous White abolitionist poet, John Greenleaf Whittier. The event illustrates that Wright, even as a boy, was not shy and was eager to be heard. Though beginning as a slave, Wright would become educator, politician, editor and banker.

Wright's probable birth year was 1855 on a Dalton, Georgia plantation. His mother, Harriet, was a house servant, and his father, Robert Waddell, was a coachman. When the boy was only 2 years old, his father escaped, and Richard and his mother were taken to Cuthbert, Georgia. His mother married Alexander Wright and gave birth to two children. But this husband, too, escaped and joined the Union Army. After the war, Harriet took her three children to Atlanta. Some reports say the family walked all the way.

In Atlanta, Richard enrolled in the American Missionary Association School, known as the "Car-Box" because it operated in an old Confederate commissary car. Later, it would be called the Storrs School. Wright was among a small group of children picked to attend the new Atlanta University, and he taught school during summers to pay for his education. In 1876, he was graduated valedictorian of his class and soon married Lydia E. Howard of Columbus, Georgia, with whom he would have five daughters and four sons.

After graduation, Wright began a life of teaching, publishing and civic involvement. He served as the first President of the Georgia State Teachers Association and organized the first public school for Blacks in Georgia. Wright also published two weekly newspapers.

In 1885, Wright received a federal appointment as a special land development agent for the Department of the Interior. He left government service when appointed president of the new State College of Industry for Colored Youth in Savannah, Georgia, where he remained for 30 years. The federal government called upon him to be minister of Liberia. Wright refused because of a sense of responsibility to his family and to the college. In 1896, however, Wright accepted a federal appointment from President William McKinley and became a paymaster in the army during the Spanish-American War.

During Wright's tenure at the college, his curiosity led him to libraries and museums, in Europe, in search of Black American involvement there. His scholarly interests led to a struggle to include classical subjects in the college's curriculum, at a time when only vocational training was considered necessary for Blacks.

In 1921, Wright left the college, and with his son Richard Jr. and his daughter Lillian, he founded a bank in Philadelphia. Aware of his inexperience in this new venture, Wright, now a senior citizen, enrolled in the University of Pennsylvania's Wharton School of Finance.

In 1945, toward the end of his life, Wright attended the San Francisco Conference, which established the United Nations. When he died two years later, in 1947, he had lived a full life, meeting three Presidents, and guiding several organizations. It was a significant record of achievement for a boy born into slavery and fatherless during much of his youth.

NOTES

TEST YOURSELF

Now that you have familiarized yourself with our *Salute to Blacks in the Federal Government* in this ninth series of Empak's Black History publications, this section, in three parts, MATCH, TRUE/FALSE, and MULTIPLE CHOICE/FILL-IN, is designed to help you remember some key points about each notable Black in the Federal Government. (Answers on page 32)

MATCH

I. *Match the column on the right with the column on the left by placing the appropriate alphabetical letter next to the person's name it represents.*

1. Henry Cheatham _____
2. Barbara Jordan _____
3. George Murray _____
4. James Rapier _____
5. Adam Clayton Powell _____
6. Edward Brooke _____
7. Archibald Grimké _____
8. James Turner _____

A) Senator from Massachusetts
B) Labor organizer
C) Counsul in Dominican Republic
D) Fought for Black Indian rights
E) Wanted Blacks in World's Fair
F) Congressional Seat from Texas
G) Spent 26 years in Congress
H) Black orphan, congressman, inventor

TRUE/FALSE

II. *The True and False statements below are taken from the biographical information given on each Black in the Federal Government.*

1. Yvonne Burke was the first Black congresswoman elected from the Deep South. _____
2. George White was the last Black Congressman of the post-Reconstruction era. _____
3. Mifflin Gibbs was the first Black elected to the U.S. House of Representatives. _____
4. Pinckney Pinchback became lieutenant-governor of Louisiana. _____
5. Ebenezer Bassett was the first Black U.S. diplomat. _____
6. Oscar DePriest was the first Black elected to the U.S. Senate. _____
7. Robert DeLarge served as consul to Liberia. _____
8. Richard Cain was an A.M.E. church bishop. _____

MULTIPLE CHOICE/FILL-IN

III. *Complete the statements below by drawing a line under the correct name, or by filling-in the correct answer which you have read in the biographical sketches.*

1. (Richard Wright, Richard Cain, Mifflin Gibbs) served 30 years as vocational college president.
2. _____ was called South Carolina's "most brilliant political organizer."
3. _____ owned 1,700 acres in Mississippi.
4. (Joseph Rainey, Yvonne Burke, Ebenezer Bassett) was the first Black seated in the U.S. House of Representatives.
5. (James Turner, Archibald Grimké, Robert Smalls) was a Civil War hero.
6. _____ received eight votes for Vice President.
7. _____ was a wounded Civil War officer.
8. _____ was the first Black on a Presidential cabinet.

CROSSWORD PUZZLE

ACROSS

1. First Black Congressman from the North
2. Louisiana Lieutenant-Governor
5. Interior Department special land agent
7. Nephew of White abolitionist sisters
9. First popularly elected Black U.S. Senator
10. Committee member for Watergate scandal hearings
11. His freedom postponed by his father's death
13. Author of a music book
16. Member of President Roosevelt's "Black Cabinet"
19. First Black U.S. diplomat
20. Prophet of Black return to Congress
21. Received 8 votes for Vice President

DOWN

1. Fighter for schools and land for the poor
2. First Black Congressman from New York
3. Also an A.M.E. Bishop
6. Consul in Madagascar
8. Farm implement inventor
12. Orphanage superintendent
13. Opposed colonization in Africa
14. Also a union leader
15. Confederate ship hijacker
17. First Black seated in U.S. House of Representatives
18. Elected to Congress from California

WORDSEARCH

1. Ebenezer D. Bassett
2. Edward W. Brooke
3. Blanche K. Bruce
4. Yvonne B. Burke
5. Richard H. Cain
6. Henry P. Cheatham
7. Robert C. DeLarge
8. Oscar S. DePriest

9. Robert B. Elliott
10. Mifflin W. Gibbs
11. Archibald H. Grimké
12. Barbara Jordan
13. John R. Lynch
14. George W. Murray
15. Pinckney B.S. Pinchback
16. Adam C. Powell, Jr.

17. Joseph H. Rainey
18. James T. Rapier
19. Robert Smalls
20. James M. Trotter
21. James M. Turner
22. Robert C. Weaver
23. George H. White
24. Richard Wright

The names of our twenty-four *BLACKS IN THE FEDERAL GOVERNMENT* are contained in the diagram below. Look in the diagram of letters for the names given in the list. Find the names by reading FORWARD, BACKWARDS, UP, DOWN, and DIAGONALLY in a straight line of letters. Each time you find a name in the diagram, circle it in the diagram and cross it off on the list of names. Words often overlap, and letters may be used more than once.

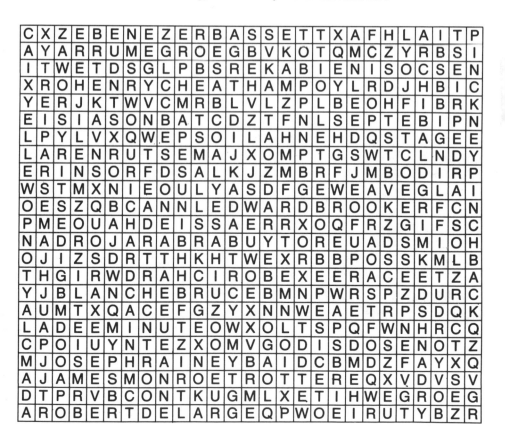

QUIZ & GAME ANSWERS

MATCH

1.–E	5.–G
2.–F	6.–A
3.–H	7.–C
4.–B	8.–D

TRUE/FALSE

1.–FALSE	5.–TRUE
2.–TRUE	6.–FALSE
3.–FALSE	7.–FALSE
4.–TRUE	8.–TRUE

MULTIPLE CHOICE/FILL-IN

1.–RICHARD WRIGHT	5.–ROBERT SMALLS
2.–ROBERT ELLIOTT	6.–BLANCHE BRUCE
3.–JOHN LYNCH	7.–JAMES MILTON TURNER
4.–JOSEPH RAINEY	8.–ROBERT WEAVER

CROSSWORD PUZZLE

WORD SEARCH

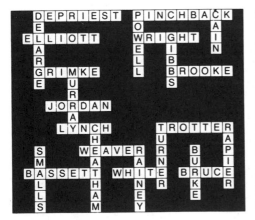

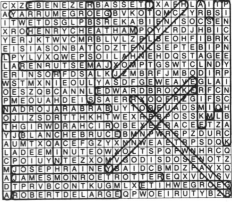

60

Send to: Empak Publishing Company, 212 E. Ohio St., Suite 300, Chicago, IL 60611—Phone: (312) 642-8364

EPC

Name _____

Affiliation _____

Address _____
P. O. Box numbers not accepted, street address must appear.

City _____ State _____ Zip _____

Phone# (_____) _____ Date _____

Method Of Payment Enclosed: ( ) Check   ( ) Money Order   ( ) Purchase Order

Prices effective 11/1/95 thru 10/31/96

ADVANCED LEVEL

Quantity	ISBN #	Title Description	Unit Price	Total Price
	0-922162-1-8	"A Salute to Historic Black Women"		
	0-922162-2-6	"A Salute to Black Scientists & Inventors"		
	0-922162-3-4	"A Salute to Black Pioneers"		
	0-922162-4-2	"A Salute to Black Civil Rights Leaders"		
	0-922162-5-0	"A Salute to Historic Black Abolitionists"		
	0-922162-6-9	"A Salute to Historic African Kings & Queens"		
	0-922162-7-7	"A Salute to Historic Black Firsts"		
	0-922162-8-5	"A Salute to Historic Blacks in the Arts"		
	0-922162-9-3	"A Salute to Blacks in the Federal Government"		
	0-922162-14-X	"A Salute to Historic Black Educators"		

INTERMEDIATE LEVEL

	0-922162-75-1	"Historic Black Women"		
	0-922162-76-X	"Black Scientists & Inventors"		
	0-922162-77-8	"Historic Black Pioneers"		
	0-922162-78-6	"Black Civil Rights Leaders"		
	0-922162-80-8	"Historic Black Abolitionists"		
	0-922162-81-6	"Historic African Kings & Queens"		
	0-922162-82-4	"Historic Black Firsts"		
	0-922162-83-2	"Historic Blacks in the Arts"		
	0-922162-84-0	"Blacks in the Federal Government"		
	0-922162-85-9	"Historic Black Educators"		

Total Books		❸ Subtotal	
	SEE ABOVE CHART ▷	❹ IL Residents add 8.75% Sales Tax	
		❺ Shipping & Handling	
GRADE LEVEL: 4th, 5th, 6th		❻ Total	

BOOK PRICING ● QUANTITY DISCOUNTS

Advanced Level	Intermediate Level
Reg. $3.49	Reg. $2.29
Order 50 or More	Order 50 or More
Save 40¢ EACH	Save 20¢ EACH
@ $3.09	@ $2.09

❺ SHIPPING AND HANDLING

Order Total	Add
Under $5.00	$1.50
$5.01-$15.00	$3.00
$15.01-$35.00	$4.50
$35.01-$75.00	$7.00
$75.01-$200.00	10%
Over $201.00	6%

In addition to the above charges, U.S. territories, HI & AK, add $2.00. Canada & Mexico, add $5.00. Other outside U.S., add $20.00.

Send to: Empak Publishing Company, 212 E. Ohio St., Suite 300, Chicago, IL 60611—Phone: (312) 642-8364

Name _____

Affiliation _____

Street _____
P. O. Box numbers not accepted, street address must appear.

City _____ State _____ Zip _____

Phone (_____)_____ Date _____

Method Of Payment Enclosed:　　( ) Check　　　　( ) Money Order　　　　( ) Purchase Order

Prices effective 11/1/95 thru 10/31/96

PRIMARY LEVEL... KINDERGARTEN, FIRST, SECOND & THIRD GRADE

Quantity	ISBN #	Title Description	Unit Price	Total Price
	0-922162-90-5	"Kumi and Chanti"		
	0-922162-91-3	"George Washington Carver"		
	0-922162-92-1	"Harriet Tubman"		
	0-922162-93-X	"Jean Baptist DuSable"		
	0-922162-94-8	"Matthew Henson"		
	0-922162-95-6	"Bessie Coleman"		

Total Books	❸ Subtotal
	❹ IL Residents add 8.75% Sales Tax
SEE CHART BELOW ▷	❺ Shipping & Handling
	❻ Total

KEY STEPS IN ORDERING

❶ Establish quantity needs.　❹ Add tax, if applicable.
❷ Determine book unit price.　❺ Add shipping &handling.
❸ Determine total cost.　❻ Total amount.

BOOK PRICING ● QUANTITY DISCOUNTS

❶ Quantity Ordered	❷ Unit Price
1-49	$3.49
50 +	$3.09

❺ SHIPPING AND HANDLING

Order Total	Add
Under $5	$1.50
$5.01-$15.00	$3.00
$15.01- $35.00	$4.50
$35.01-$75.00	$7.00
$75.01-$200.00	10%
Over $201.00	6%

In addition to the above charges, U.S. territories, HI & AK, add $2.00. Canada and Mexico, add $5.00. Other outside U.S., add $20.00.

Empak Publishing provides attractive counter and floor displays for retailers and organizations interested in the Heritage book series for resale. Please check here ☐ and include this form with your letterhead and we will send you specific information and our special volume discounts.

- The Empak "Heritage Kids" series provides a basic understanding and appreciation of Black history which translates to cultural awareness, self-esteem, and ethnic pride within young African-American children.

- Assisted by dynamic and impressive 4-color illustrations, readers will be able to relate to the two adorable African kids -- Kumi & Chanti, as they are introduced to the inspirational lives and deeds of significant, historic African-Americans.

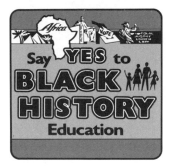

Black History Materials
Available from Empak Publishing

A Salute To Black History Poster Series
African-American Experience–Period Poster Series
Biographical Poster Series
Heritage Kids Poster Series

Advanced Booklet Series
Instructor's Manuals
Advanced Skills Sheets
Black History Bulletin Board Aids
Instructor's Kits

Intermediate Booklet Series
Teacher's Guides
Intermediate Skill Sheets
Black History Flashcards
Intermediate Reading Certificates
Teacher's Kits

Heritage Kids Booklet Series
Heritage Kids Resource & Activity Guides
Heritage Kids Reading Certificates
Heritage Kids Kits

Black History Videos
Black History Month Activity & Resource Guide
African-American Times–A Chronological Record
African-American Discovery Board Game
African-American Clip Art
Black History Mugs
Black Heritage Marble Engraving
Black History Month Banners (18" x 60")
Say YES to Black History Education Sweatshirts
Say YES to Black History Education T-Shirts

To receive your copy of the Empak Publishing Company's
colorful new catalog, please send $2 to cover postage and handling to:

Empak Publishing Company
Catalog Dept., Suite 300
212 East Ohio Street
Chicago, IL 60611